MATHEMATICS OF FINANCE

Toye Adelaja

TABLE OF CONTENTS

TIME VALUE OF MONEY

Financial decisions recognize that money has value over time. This means that an amount of money now, has a greater value than the same amount at some time in the future. This idea is based on the fact that if you have $x now, you can make it to work for you so that you obtain $x plus in the future. Given this situation, lenders of money would also want to be compensated financially for sacrificing their present consumption. The amount they received in the future is known as interest. It should be noted that this interest will be charged even if no inflation is anticipated and it is certain that the money will be received.

1.1 INTEREST

Interest, like commodity price in the commodity markets, is the price one pays for money in the financial markets. It is that vital factor that is used to quantify the time value of money. Interest rate makes possible the conversion of the values of cash flows having different timings to a desired point in time; for the purpose of financial decision-making. Thus, present values, with the aid of interest rate can be converted to future values and vice versa.

There are many types of interest rates. Some of them are explained below:

1.1.2. Nominal Interest Rate is the commonest and simplest type of interest rate. It is the interest rate lenders normally quote in loan and deposit agreements. It is the actual monetary price that borrowers pay to lenders for the use of their funds or money.

Nominal interest rate is the interest rate that is inclusive of inflation if there is any. For instance, an investor is offered a 6% interest rate on a deposit, and inflation is running at 2%. The rate of return that is available to the investor is 4%. The 4% is the real rate of interest while 6% is the nominal rate of interest.

1.1.3　Real Rate of Interest is the rate of interest that excludes inflation. Real rate of interest = Nominal rate of interest – inflation rate

1.1.4.　Effective Rate of Interest is the true rate of interest you pay on loan or you earn on your savings. The effective rate of interest is calculated as if compounded annually.

The effective rate of interest can be calculated using the formula below:

$Er = (1 + r/n)^n - 1$

Where:

"Er" represents effective rate of interest, "n" represents the number of times in which interest is compounded annually, "r"represents nominal rate.

Example 1

A nominal rate of interest is 6% per annum and compounded monthly. What is the effective rate of interest?

$Er = (1 + r/n)^n - 1$

$\quad = (1 + 0.06/12)^{12} - 1$

$\quad = 0.061677$

$\quad = 0.0617$

$\quad = 0.0617 \times 100$

$\quad = 6.17\%$

The effective rate of interest is 6.17%.

The effective interest rate can be used to multiply capital invested to get the actual amount of interest. For instance, if an investor invests $1,000 and the rate of interest is 6% per annum and compounded monthly. What is the interest?

$1,000 × 6.17% = $61.7

The interest is $61.7.

Chapter 2

SIMPLE INTEREST AND COMPOUND INTEREST

2.1. SIMPLE INTEREST

The **simple interest** is the earnings on an original amount invested (principal). The amount of principal and the interest payments remain the same from period to period.
The simple interest is (S.I) computed as:

$$\text{S.I} = \frac{\text{Principal} \times \text{Rate} \times \text{Time}}{100} \quad \text{or} \quad \frac{P \times R \times T}{100}$$

$$P = \frac{100 \times \text{S.I}}{RT}$$

Principal is the original money invested. Rate of Interest is the % at which principal will increase. Time is the number of years in which the principal will be invested.

Example: What is the Simple Interest on $2,000 invested for 4 years at the rate of 5% per annum?

Year	Principal ($)	Rate of Interest	Interest (P×R) $
1	2,000	5%	100
2	2,000	5%	100
3	2,000	5%	100
4	2,000	5%	100
	S.I		400

The Simple Interest is $400.

Formula can also be used to calculate S.I. This is faster than the use of table.

$$\text{S.I} = \frac{P \times R \times T}{100}$$
$$= \frac{2,000 \times 5 \times 4}{100}$$
$$= \$400$$

2.2. COMPOUND INTEREST

As against simple interest, where interest is charged on the principal only for the relevant period, compound interest is charged and added to the principal from period to period; both principal and interest forming the basis of the next period interest calculation. The compound interest is the periodic interest earned on the principal plus previous earned interest.

Compound interest can be computed using formula or table:
 Compound Interest = Total sum of money available at the end of the investment – Initial Principal Invested

Example: What is the compound Interest on $2,000 invested by Mr. Stone for 4 years at the rate of 5% per annum?

Solution:
Computation of compound interest using table:

Years	Principal $	Returns $	Rate	Cumulative amount $ (P+Return)
1	2,000	100	5%	2,100
2	2,100	105	5%	2,205
3	2,205	110.25	5%	2,315.25
4	2,315.25	115.76	5%	2,431.01

Compound Interest = $2,431.01 – $2,000
$$= \$431.01$$
The total amount of money available to Mr. Stone is $2,431.01 at the end of 4th year. The total return on his investment is $ 431.01.

Computation by the use of formula:

$$A = P(1+r)^n$$

Where:

A= Total Sum
P= Initial cash invested
r = rate of interest

n= number of years

Solution to the question:

Total sum expected $= P(1+r)^4$
$$= 2,000(1+0.05)^4$$
$$= \$2,431.01$$
Compound Interest $= 2,431.01 - 2,000$
$$= \$431.01$$

2.2.1. Future Value of a Lump Sum

Meaning of time value of money has already been explained in the previous studies.
Some further studies on time value of money will be considered here.
One important area in which compound interest principles can be applied is where a single lump sum is deposited, for example, in fixed deposit or savings account at a specified rate of interest per period. This deposit is allowed to grow undisturbed while the interest is assumed to be re-invested.

The future lump sum of the amount invested today can be computed as:

$$FV = P(1+r)^n$$

Where, FV = future value of a lump sum
P = present value
r = rate of return
n = number of years of the investment

ILLUSTRATION 1

Mr. Smith invested $2,000 in a fixed deposit account for 3 years at the rate of 11 per cent per annum. If the amount is left untouched, what will be the worth of investment at the end of the third year?

SUGGESTED SOLUTION:

$$FV = P(1+r)^n$$
$$= \$2,000(1+0.11)^3$$
$$= \$2,735.26$$

The worth of the investment at the end of third year is $2,735.26

ILLUSTRATION 2

If, interest on the above investment of $2,000 is to be compounded monthly (instead of once in the year), given 11 per cent as the rate of interest, what will be the value at the end of one year?

SUGGESTED SOLUTION

The appropriate formula for calculating this value will be:

$$FV_n = P(1+r/m)^{mn}$$

The modification in the compound interest formula has already been dealt with in the previous studies of "time value of money"
$$FV = \$2,000(1+0.11/12)^{12\times1}$$
$$FV = \$2,231.44$$

ILLUSTRATION 3

Assume an amount of $2,000 is put in a fixed deposit account for 10 years at the rate of 12% per cent per annum. If the amount is left untouched, what will be the investment at the end of tenth year?

SOLUTION:

$$FV_n = P(1+r)^n$$

$$FV_{10} = \$2,000(1+0.12)^{10}$$

$$= \$6,211.7$$

The investment will be $6,211.7 at the end of the tenth year.

Where:

FV_{10} represents total sum expected at the end of year 10.

2.2.2 Frequency of Compounding

There are some investments in which the interest is compounded for more than once in a year.

Multiple compounding within a year increases the effective interest rate, assuming interest is compounding "m" times during the year.

Adjustments in Compound Interest formula are as follows:

$A = P (1 + r/m)^{mn}$
m = number of compounding periods

This formula is applicable where the number of time in which interest is compounding is more than once in a year. Examples:

Where interest is compounding semi-annually; $A = (1 + r/2)^{2n}$
Where interest is compounding quarterly ; $A = (1 + r/4)^{4n}$
Where interest is compounding monthly ; $A = (1 + r/12)^{12n}$

ILLUSTRATION 1

Mr, Stone invested $2,000 in a fixed deposit account for one year at the rate of 12 per cent per annum. The rate is to be compounded monthly. You are required:
1) To calculate the worth of the investment at the end of one year
2) Calculate the effective rate of interest.

SOLUTION

1) $FV_1 = P(1+r/m)^{mn}$

    $= \$2,000 \, (1 + 0.12/12)^{12 \times 1}$

    $= \$2,253.65$

2) Effective rate of interest:

$Er = (1 + r/m)^{mn} - 1$

  $= (1 + 0.12/12)^{12 \times 1} - 1$

  $= (1.01)^{12} - 1$

  $= 1.1268 - 1$

  $= 0.1268$

  $= 12.68\%$

2.2.3. Continuous Compounding

This is a situation in which the number of times in a year in which the interest compounds approaches infinity. It is a circumstance where compounding periods are infinitely short.

It can be represented by the formula below:

$FV_n = P_0 \, (e^{r \times n})$

"e" is the symbol for irrational number 2.71828

ILLUSTRATION

What is the value at the end of three years of $2,000 deposited at 12 percent per annum with interest compound continuously?

SOLUTION

$$FV_n = P_0 (e^{r \times n})$$

$$FV_3 = P_0 (e^{0.12 \times 3})$$

$$= \$2,000 \times (2.71828^{0.36})$$

$$= \$2,866.66$$

The maximum value of $2,000 at the end of 3 years is $2,866.66.

2.2.4. Future Value with Regular Annual Investment

In this situation, there is an initial deposit with an addition of a fixed amount at the end of each period. The future value can be arrived at by the use of the following formula:

$$FV_n = (P_0 + p/r)(1 + r)^n - p/r$$

Where "p" is the regular additional investment which is assumed to be made at the end of each period.

ILLUSTRATION

An investor made an initial deposit of $25,000 at the beginning of 2007. While this amount remained invested, he plans to be adding $2,500 0n January 1 each subsequent year starting from January 1 2008. Assuming that interest is compounded each year at the rate of 12 per cent per annum, what will be the value of his investment on January 1, 2011?

SUGGESTED SOLUTION

$FV_n = (P_0 + p/r)(1 + r)^n - p/r$

$\quad = (25{,}000 + 2{,}500/0.12)(1+0.12)^4 - 2{,}500/0.12$

$\quad = (45833)(1.5735) - 20833.33)$

$\quad = \$72{,}118 - \$2{,}0833.33$

$\quad = \$51{,}284.67$

2.2.5. Regular Annual Withdrawals

If "p" is allowed to be negative, the same formula can be used to calculate the amount that will be left from an initial investment given withdrawal of regular fixed amount at the end of each period.

ILLUSTRATION 1

A Pensioner deposits \$20,000 representing his gratuity in a bank account and withdraws \$3,000 at the end of each year beginning from the end of the first year. What will be the balance of his bank account after five years if the deposit is invested at 12 percent per annum?

SUGGESTED SOLUTION

$FV_n = (P_0 - p/r)(1 + r)^n + p/r$

$\quad = (20{,}000 - 3{,}000/0.12)(1+0.12)^5 + 3{,}000/0.12$

$\quad = (20{,}000 - 25{,}000)(1.7623) + 25{,}000$

$\quad = \$33{,}811.5$

The balance of his bank account after five years will be \$33,811.5.

2.2.6. Present Value of a Future Lump Sum

A present value of an investment can be described as the amount of money (a lump sum) that you would have to invest now for "n" time periods earning interest at "r" per time period, to build up the value of your investment to $FV at the end of that time.

$$P = F (1+ r)^{-n} \quad OR \quad P = \frac{F \times 1}{(1+ r)^{n}}$$

ILLUSTRATION 1

Mrs. Macdon wants to know how much she can invest now to earn $2,735.26 in 3 years if the interest is compounding at 11% annually.

SUGGESTED SOLUTION

$P = FV (1 + r)^{-n}$
$P = \$2,735.26 (1+ 0.11)^{-3}$
$P = \$2,735.26 \times 0.731191381$
$P = \$ 1,999.9985$
$P = \$2,000$

Mrs. Macdon will have to invest approximately, $2,000 to earn $2,735.26 in 3years, given the above compound interest.

ILLUSTARATION 2:

Mr. John wants to invest $10,000 now at 8 percent per annum compounded annually. He wants this amount to become $20,000. Approximately, how long will the investment take, for him to realize this amount?

SUGGESTED SOLUTION:

$20,000 = 10,000(1 + 0.08)^{n}$

$$\frac{20,000}{10,000} = \frac{10,000}{10,000}(1 + 0.08)^n$$

$$2 \quad = 1(1.08)^n$$

$$\log 2 \quad = \log 1.08^n$$

$$\log 2 \quad = n\log 1.08$$

$$0.3010 = n \times 0.0334$$

$$\frac{0.3010}{0.0334} = \frac{n \times 0.0334}{0.0334}$$

$$9.012 \quad = n$$

$$n \quad = 9.012$$

$$n \quad = 9 \text{ years}$$

Approximately, the investment will take 9 years to realize $20,000

Chapter 3

ANNUITY

An annuity is a series of equal payments or receipt over some periods, with compound interest on the payments or receipts. We can divide annuity into ordinary annuity and annuity due.

3.1. Ordinary Annuity Formula

This is a series of equal payments or receipts that occur at the end of each period involved.

Future Value

$$FV = \frac{A\,[(1+r)^n - 1)]}{r}$$

Present Value

$$PV = \frac{A\,[(1-(1+)^{-n}]}{r}$$

Where,

FV is the future value of the ordinary annuity.

A is the equal amount to be paying or receiving at the end of each period.

r is the rate of compound interest.

n is the number of years of the payment or receipt.

PV is the present value of the ordinary annuity.

3.1.1. FUTURE VALUE OF AN ANNUITY (ORDINARY)

ILLUSTRATION 1

Assume you take up a savings program asking for deposit of $10,000 at the end of each year for the next three years in an account paying 12 percent per annum compounded annually. How much will you have in the account at the end of the third year?

SUGGESTED SOLUTION

$$FV = \frac{A\,[(1+r)^n - 1)]}{r}$$

$$= \frac{10,000[(1+0.12)^3 - 1)]}{0.12}$$

$$= \frac{10,000[(1.4049 - 1)]}{0.12}$$

$$= \frac{10,000[(0.4049)]}{0.12}$$

$$= \$33,741.66$$

The amount that you will be having in the account at the end of third year is $33,741.66.

3.1.2. PRESENT VALUE OF ORDINARY ANNUITY

The formula for calculating present value of ordinary annuity is:

$$PV = \frac{A\,[1-(1+r)^{-n}]}{r}$$

ILLUSTRATION 1

Assume you take up a savings program asking for deposit of $10,000 at the end of each year for the next three years in an account paying

12 percent per annum compounded annually. Calculate the present value of this annuity.

$$PV = \frac{A[1-(1+r)^{-n}]}{r}$$

$$PV = \frac{10,000[1-(1+0.12)^{-3}]}{0.12}$$

$$PV = \frac{10,000[1-(1.12)^{-3}]}{0.12}$$

$$PV = \frac{\$2,882.20}{0.12}$$

$$PV = \$24,018$$

The present value of the ordinary annuity is $24,018.

3.2. Annuity Due

Annuity due is a series of payments or receipts that occur at the beginning of each period involved.

3.2.1. Future Value of an Annuity Due

$$FVd = A\frac{(1+r)^n - 1)(1+r)}{r}$$

ILLUSTRATION 1

Assume you take up a savings program asking for deposit of $10,000 at the beginning of each year for the next three years in an account paying 12 percent per annum compounded annually. Calculate the present value of this annuity.

$$FVd = A\frac{(1+r)^n - 1)(1+r)}{r}$$

$$FVd = \frac{10,000[1- (1+ 0.12)^{-3}](1+0.12)}{0.12}$$

$$\frac{10,000[(1+ 0.12)^3 - 1)](1.12)}{0.12}$$

$$= \frac{10,000[(1.4049 - 1)](1.12)}{0.12}$$

$$= \frac{10,000[(0.4049)](1.12)}{0.12}$$

$$= \$33,741.66(1.12)$$

$$= \$37,790.66$$

3.3. Concept of Perpetual Annuity

Perpetual Annuity is described as a situation in which constant sum of money is saved or withdraw for an indefinite time.

The formula for calculating present value of perpetual annuity is described below:

$$Pv = A \times 1/r$$

Where:

Pv = Present value of annuity
A = The constant or equal annual sum
r = rate of interest or cost of capital

ILLUSTRATION

Calculate the present value of $1,000 receivable every year for indefinite period at the interest rate of 10% per annum.

$$Pv = A \times 1/r$$
$$= \$1,000 \times 1/0.1$$

= $10,000

Chapter 4

Application of Annuity to Business Decision

4.1. Sinking Funds

Sinking fund is a method of setting aside uniform amount at every period to accumulate to a specific amount in the future. As each periodic amount is set aside, it will be immediately invested. This is what we call a sinking fund. It can be used in providing for replacement of fixed assets.

ILLUSTRATION 1

Mr. Joe needs to provide $50,000 to replace his machine in 5 years time, in order to provide this amount he decides to set aside equal amount annually, out of his salary. This amount is kept in savings account that yield 20% interest per annum. Find this amount, and the sinking fund schedule.

SOLUTION

The calculation of each amount that will be kept aside annually to meet this need is:

$$FV = \frac{A\,[(1+r)^n - 1)]}{r}$$

$$\$50,000 = \frac{A\,[(1+0.2)^5 - 1)]}{0.2}$$

$$\$50,000 \times 0.2 = A(1.2)^5 - 1$$

$$\$10,000 = A(2.4883 - 1)$$

$$\$10,000 = A \times 1.4883$$

$$\frac{\$10,000}{1.4883} = A$$

$6,719 = A$

The amount that will be kept aside annually is $6,719

Sinking Fund Schedule:

Years	a Balance b/f	b Interest $	c Sinking Fund $	a+b+c Balance c/d $
1			6,719.00	6,719.00
2	6,719.00	1,343.80	6,719.00	14,781.80
3	14,781.80	2,956.36	6,719.00	24,457.16
4	24,457.16	4,891.43	6,719.00	36,067.59
5	36,067.59	7,213.52	6,719.00	50,000.11

The sinking fund for each year is $6,719

4.2. Loan Amortization

This is a method of payment of loan, which includes both principal amount and interest spread over a period of time. Installment payments are common in certain types of business loans and mortgage loans. The main characteristic of installment payments is that the borrower repays the loan in equal period payments that include both principal and interest. The series of equal payments is an example of **annuity**.

Annuity is a series of equal payments or receipts over some periods, with compound interests on the payments or receipts. Annuity can be divided into ordinary annuity and annuity due.

Illustration

AAT Company Ltd. borrowed $5,000 to purchase a machine. He made arrangement to pay over 5 years period with interest rate of 2% per month on the unpaid balance.

You are required to:

      i.Calculate the monthly payment.

      ii.Prepare loan amortization schedule.

  Solution:

$$PV = \frac{A(1-(1+r)^{-n})}{r}$$

$$5{,}000 = \frac{A(1-(1+0.02)^{-5})}{0.02}$$

$$5{,}000 = \frac{A(1-0.9057)}{0.02}$$

$$5{,}000 \times 0.02 = A(0.0943)$$

$100 = A(0.0943)$

$100/0.0943 = A$

$A = 1,060.45$

Note:

A = Annual repayment

PV = Present value

r = interest charged per month

Mon-ths	Amounts owing $	Interest payments $	Principal payments $	Installment payments $	Balance $
0					5,000.00
1	5,000.00	100.00	960.45	1,060.45	4,039.55
2	4,039.55	80.79	979.65	1,060.45	3,059.90
3	3,059.90	61.20	999.25	1,060.45	2,060.65
4	2,060.65	41.22	1,019.23	1,060.45	1,041.43
5	1,041.43	20.82	1,039.63	1,060.45	1.80
	Total	304.03	4,998.20	5,302.23	

The total interest should be $302.23 and not $304.03. The $304.03 was arrived at as a result of rounding figure. The installment for each period is $5,302.23

REREFERENCES:

www.accountinghour.com

Toye Adelaja (2015) – Capital Budgeting

www.ingramcontent.com/pod-product-compliance
Lightning Source LLC
Chambersburg PA
CBHW070928180526
45168CB00005B/2194